HUNG BY THE TONGUE

HUNG BY THE TONGUE

by
Francis P. Martin

*For Bible Teaching seminars, books, and tapes
contact:*

Francis P. Martin
Bible Teaching Seminars, Books and Tapes
P.O. Box 52444
Lafayette, Louisiana 70505
(318) 988-0030

Copyright 1979 by Francis P. Martin

Previous ISBN: 0-89858-014-5
Current ISBN: 0-9652433-0-3

Published by
F.P.M. PUBLICATIONS
P. O. Box 52444
Lafayette, LA 70505

Printed and bound by
Offset Paperback Mfrs., Inc.
Dallas, Pennsylvania

FOREWORD

By John F. Stephens, Ph.D.

An insatiable interest in how things work led me
to enter the mechanical engineering program at the
University of Cincinnati after graduation from high
school. The field of engineering fascinated me to
the point where I spent ten years in study finally
earning my Ph.D. Of all the machines studied, the
human body absolutely amazed me; how did the
various parts function, how did they interact with
each other, what caused body malfunctions and
disease? Intrigued by this, the most complex of all
machines, I spent four more years studying the
field of cardiology in the hope that I could help
answer these questions about the heart, lungs, and
other parts of the circulatory system. For years
medical research became my chief interest as I
tried to add to man's knowledge of the causes and
cures of disease and bodily malfunction.

During the early part of 1976, my wife and I
were filled with the Holy Spirit, thus ushering in an
entirely new dimension in living. It was fascinating
to learn after so many years of study that all sickness is Satanic oppression (Acts 10:38). Even more
surprising was the realization that the Lord God
Almighty wants to be our mighty physician and to
meet all of our medical needs. Believers can lay

their hands on the sick and they will recover (Mark 16:18)—"Fantastic," I thought; "teach me more." Luke 10:19 taught me that I had authority over **all** the power of the enemy; Galatians 4:7 says that I **am** a son of God and therefore not entitled to **any** defeat at the hands of the enemy.

In my learning experience, my question at this point was obviously—"If I am not entitled to it, and the enemy has no authority over me, then how come sometimes I am defeated?" Finally I learned that the secret is in the tongue. Satan only has authority over us when we give him that authority with our mouth. **Hung by the Tongue**, then, contains the essential implementing facts of the truly victorious Christian life; namely, how to control our tongue.

As an illustration of the power of the tongue, let me cite some recent medical findings that presently baffle physicians. The heart attack is this nation's number one killer of adults. Until recently, researchers thought that the flow of blood to the heart itself was slowly cut off by a clot in the coronary artery, thus producing the heart attack. Recent research, however, has established the fact that the clot forms **after** the onset of all the symptoms. I firmly believe that the enemy (Satan) gives the symptoms of a heart attack to some unsuspecting person and after physicians diagnose these symptoms as a heart attack, the person becomes "hung by the tongue" and truly has a heart attack.

Please read this book carefully—the secret to the victorious Christian life is in the mouth—the principles of controlling our tongue are contained herein.

Cover Design and Art — Batson Trahan

Contents

Introduction

The first statement I want to make is: "What You Say is What You Get." The scripture reference is Mark 11:23. That's exactly what it says. "Do you see this mountain? If you want to move it, all you have to do is speak to it and if you will believe what you say, then you can have it. You can have whatsoever you say." These are true words, these are scriptural words: "what you say is what you get." It's not as the famous TV comedian would say, "what you *see* is what you get," because we don't walk by sight, we walk by faith.

This is a study of controlling the words of your mouth. Why do you want to control the words of your mouth? The words of your mouth have control of your life, whether you *like it or not*, or whether you *believe it or not*. We have found this to be true. What comes out of your mouth will determine your future. We have always said that God knows the future—is that right? Well, how does He know it? Because He is God? There is more to it than that. God knows the future because He has *spoken* the future. You see, He spoke the world into existence and He spoke everything else into existence. He spoke the future into existence, He said, "this world will pass away but my *Word* will never pass away." When you speak about predestination, consider this: "God is not willing that any should perish." If you ask, "Does God *know* whether I am going to be saved or not?'', I will answer, ''I do not know.'' God spoke that you *should* have redemption, and you have it if you *want* it. God *spoke* the future. That is why He *knows* the future. He also put *your* future into *your* hands, so that YOU CAN SPEAK your salvation or your future. That may sound strange. You may not have heard that before, but you actually *speak your own future*. That is why I am training myself to control my words, to control my future. Your words are spirit and life—once you speak them, they become life. We are going to show you within the pages of this book how exactly *what you say is what you get*.

The second thing I want you to consider is this. You cannot rise above what you allow yourself to think or say. You can think back, and as you think about your past life, the life you have been leading, ask yourself this question: ''What has been happening to me?'' Then stop and think about what you have been saying or thinking all of your life. You will find that you have been speaking your life into existence. Now I have not given you any basis for this so far, but in this book you are going to see how this is true. You are going to be convicted in your heart, because we will give you enough scripture to show you this.

So, at this point, stop, and open your mind and spirit to Jesus Christ our Lord and ask the Father to teach you His ways.

Chapter I

The Words of Your Mouth Begin with Thinking

To control your mouth, you must control your mind. Right and wrong thinking is the basis for controlling your words. Prov. 23:7 — "As (a man) thinketh in his heart, so is he." The Bible means exactly what it says — a man is what he thinks. You *must* accept the "literacy" of scripture. Prov. 23:7 *states a spiritual principle*. The basic difference between a spiritual principle and a man-made law is, that which God set forth cannot be broken. It is always operative. A man-made law, however, can be broken at will. A "no-smoking" law can be broken by the simple act of lighting up a cigarette.

A spiritual principle such as the *law of sowing and reaping* can never be broken. This spiritual principle always works. Luke 6:37-38 tells us that whatever we give out, we will have it multiplied back to us. If you criticize people, you will reap criticism. If you judge people, you will be judged. If you bless people, you will receive blessing in return.

The Laws of Physics which Man has discovered are dependable at all times. These are very valuable in charting a course by the stars, when sailing, or launching a rocket to the moon and returning to earth. We can depend on God's principles. Now let's quote again one of God's principles: "As a man thinketh in his heart, so is he." Will you, dear reader, recognize this moment that this principle is operating in your life, that it has been the basic controlling factor in your life up to this time and it *will* be in the future? God will prosper you as you submit yourself to His principles.

1. The Root of Thinking—Thoughts

How do you begin to think? Where does your thinking start? The answer is, your thinking starts with thoughts. Is that right? I put it that way so you could start elementarily looking at what you have been doing.

In counseling, I deal with many people whose minds are running wild, so badly that I cannot talk to them. Sometimes I have to tell them to *shut up*. I have to shut them up and tell them to forget everything that they know. I have to shut them up because their minds are "running" too much. What causes your mind to run wild? A bombardment of thoughts.

The Origin of Thoughts

There are three sources from which we receive thoughts. First, thoughts come from your five senses. Everything you have learned since you were born into this world, everything your mind has learned, has entered through your five senses. Therefore, we know that thoughts come through your five senses, either from your present environment, or what you have stored in your subconscious mind. You might just be doing nothing one day and a thought *hits* you. That thought could be from something you have learned a long time ago. It is in your subconscious mind. That is one way a thought can come.

A second source from which a thought can come is the devil. Satan can bombard your mind with thoughts. We know this because the scripture supports it. John 13:2—"The devil put the thought of betrayal into Judas' heart." Judas conjured up the plan that He was going to betray Jesus. Maybe Judas thought he was doing right; however, he received that thought into his mind. Now, when did he start thinking about this? The Bible says the devil put the thought of betrayal into his mind. We see then, that your thinking upon a particular line of reasoning can be started by the devil placing a thought in your mind. Later we will show you that Satan cannot *read* your mind, only *attack* your mind. We qualify this also by saying that you are protecting yourself from ESP, telepathy and the like. Do not place yourself on Satan's battleground.

Third, God can also put thoughts into your heart and mind by His Holy Spirit. Now, the *main difference* between thoughts that come from the five senses and the thoughts that come from God is this: God deals with your *spirit* and the other deals with your *mind*. Romans 8:7 says that the natural mind alone or the sensual part of you cannot know God. God speaks to you through your spirit and your spirit speaks to your mind. Whether or not your mind can use the thoughts is based on whether or not your mind is renewed by the Word of God according to Romans 12:2.

2. The Mind is a Machine—Like a Computer

How can you tell what thoughts are good or bad? You must *program* your "computer" or mind. This is what Romans 12:2 is saying, getting your mind renewed to the Word of God. Your mind is a computer or machine, and knows nothing except what it has been fed. Your heart or spirit is the *real* you from where the issues of life flow.

Now, what do you do with a computer? You have a machine that is brand new and knows nothing. The things that you want the machine to know is what you feed into it. You decide what you want a computer to remember and that is the data you feed into it. That is what has been happpening to you since you were born. You have been "programmed" by your particular circumstances, or the world that you have been living in. "Be not conformed to this world, have your mind renewed by the Word of God." (Romans 12:2). Actually, we are going to have to *re-program* our minds instead of just programming them.

Now, trying to re-program your mind is like un-pickling pickles. Have you ever tried to un-pickle a pickle? That is the job we have on our hands, to get these old worldly minds renewed by the Word of God. When you come into divine healing, you say, "Well, I will start trusting God more," and you will begin releasing the *natural ways* or *man's ways*. When you start believing God for healing, then you do not have to use man's ways. It is like that in every situation in your Christian life. You get your mind thinking scripturally. You can realize now that you *have* to be very selective as thoughts continue to bombard your mind from these three sources. Your mind will accept or reject thoughts according to what it knows about the Word of God.

Learn to use the Word of God. Read Psalm 119 and as you read through it, underline every place where it says "Thy Word" or "Thy Precepts." The Psalmist was talking about God's ways and as you get lined up with God's ways you will protect yourself.

You protect your mind and you start thinking

like God thinks. I Cor. 2:16, "We have the mind of Christ." Many Christians have been brought up thinking that *"God works in strange and mysterious ways His wonders to perform."* Many people will quote this scripture, but it is not in God's Word. The Bible actually says the opposite, "We have the mind of Christ." I Cor. 2 says that God's Spirit is within us and reveals to us the things that God has prepared for us. Matt. 13:11 says, "It has been given to you to know the mysteries of Heaven and not to them (the unbelievers)." Eph. 1:9 says, "Having made known unto us the mystery of His will." *PLEASE REALIZE,* we can and must think like God thinks—according to His word and not according to how we were trained. That is why He gave you His word. Psalm 119:105 says, "Thy Word is a lamp unto my feet, a light unto my path." You are going to take the Word of God and use it as a base on which you operate your mind. These are all elementary things that we have to settle on before we go to anything else. Proverbs 3:5 says, "Lean not unto your own understanding." We must trust God's ways for our decisions; as we go through life, there are decisions to make. Many times we decide by relating to past experiences or the experiences of other people rather than God's Word. This is not a secure foundation. Some people seek help from fortune tellers, seers and other so-called psychics, which is forbidden to the

Christian by scripture.

In the administration of church business, more so than not, decisions are made by the board or congregation according to what they are used to doing. They will say, "We have never done that in that fashion in *this* church." What they are really saying is this: "Sorry, God, you cannot change our way of doing things."

While we are on this point, permit me to offer the following, even at the chance of being called a heretic. I have found through experience, that it is better to have one pastor as head of a fellowship than to have a board or group to vote on a decision. (God gives a ministry to a *man* not to a group.) Providing that man will seek God, study His Word and be willing to hear from God, God can speak His plan to the one man. On the other hand, if there are six on the board, they might be concerned with other things of life and not find time to seek God. Therefore, when the pastor brings up a revelation of direction that he has received from God, many times the plan of God is voted down by man's own understanding. That is why we must open our mind and say, "I do not care which way God goes, I want to go with Him. Therefore, I have to quit thinking in my natural ways and I have to start thinking the way God does." This is what we are opening ourselves to. We will have our minds programmed by the Word of God.

3. After Re-programming, Censor Thoughts

You may have read the scripture, II Cor. 10:5, many times. It says, "casting down imaginations (or reasonings) and every high thing that exalteth itself against the knowledge of God." How can something come against the knowledge of God? This is the battleground—right in your mind. You have the Word of God coming into your heart and the devil putting thoughts into your mind against the knowledge of God. The Bible says here that you must cast down every imagination or reasoning that exalts itself against the knowledge of God. As your mind is programmed with the Word of God, then anything that comes against the Word of God will be cast down. That is what you must do with thoughts because every day you will run into this problem. Every time you get into a conversation with anyone, if you are not talking about the Word of God, then you are going to face this. You must train yourself in this area and God's Holy Spirit will check you. He will keep you straight. The Bible says to bring every thought captive unto the obedience of Christ. You take those thoughts we were talking about, those thoughts that are given to you by your surroundings, your five senses, by Satan, or by God; you take all of them and bring them captive unto the obedience of Christ, the Bible says. Every thought that comes into my mind, I say, has to come into obedience to Christ, because I am living the Jesus-type life and because I have the Word of God in me. I ask of every thought—does it line up with scripture? If it doesn't, I throw it out. To do this, I must know the scripture. That is why Romans 12:2 says to get your mind renewed. You have to program your mind with the Word of God.

Our scripture speaks of thoughts, imaginations and strongholds. What are the differences between these? Thoughts are the initial thing. The thought coming into your mind—that is the initial data. After the thought comes, then you must decide what you are going to do with it. If it is a bad thought, it would be dangerous to dwell on it. That is what Judas Iscariot did. "Betray Jesus? Oh, no, I would never betray my Master." "Now wait a minute, if I betray Him, let's see," and Judas starts thinking about that. "If I could betray Him, then the Jews or the Christians would come to rescue Him and make Him King." Judas starts imagining what could happen. The thought turns into an imagination. After he imagines too long, the imagination turns into a stronghold and the stronghold starts controlling his life. The Bible says we have power to pull down these strongholds. When the thought comes, we do not let it become an imagination. If it is bad, if it is against God, we throw it out.

You can deal this way in every area of your life. You can do it in the financial realm and in business. You can do it in every area of your personal life. If you do not let the thought become imaginations they will not become strongholds, because the Bible says that as a man thinketh in his heart, so is he.

Thoughts are the *original ideas,* imaginations are *the image,* and strongholds are a *result of thoughts that come to reality.* The stronghold is what controls you if you allow it to. Jesus has given you authority over your thinking, but you have to *take* authority, and *stay* in authority. It is an act of your will.

An imagination is an intent to do something about what you have been thinking; a stronghold is when the choice is not yours anymore, but you have submitted your will to the thought.

For example, the thought of suicide comes to your mind. You can decide to dismiss the thought or keep it. If you choose to keep the thought and dwell upon it, the thought will become an imagination or an intention to commit suicide. If you leave it as an imagination, it will grow into a stronghold and you will be going into the act of suicide with no power to turn back, except you submit that thing to the power of God and pull it down in the name and authority of Jesus' name.

Col. 3:15, ''Let the peace of God rule in your

hearts." Don't let frustration, fear or anger rule your heart, but give the reign to the peace of God. Let all thoughts become subject to the peace that God has put into your heart.

Whenever a thought comes and you cannot follow that line of thinking in the peace of God, then you should dismiss it. Direction for you that is produced by God will not disturb the peace of God within your spirit. If your mind is not renewed by the Word of God, then your *natural mind* might rebel, as sometimes the flesh wants to rebel to God's plans. Therefore, your mind will be ruled by the peace of God instead of thoughts, imaginations and strongholds of the enemy.

Psychosomatics Are People Who Have Developed Sicknesses From Thoughts

This is something we all know about—one who thinks he is sick. Now they really do develop physical sickness, it's true, if they think on it long enough. Professional doctors will support this. Many of their beds are filled with people who have become physically sick because they started thinking they were sick. It goes so far as this: there are some in the hospital that doctors are trying to send home but they will not go home. Doctors are trying to get them off of medicine, but they refuse. They have to have medication or sugar pills, because that thought has become a stronghold. They say, "I am sick, I have *got* to be sick."

I will now offer a personal testimony on this subject. Two years after I was saved, I read a little booklet about a disease. After reading the book, I started looking at my own body for symptoms. As time went on, I began to find or manufacture symptoms according to the thoughts produced by the book. I was starting to accept the disease into my body. Through constant worry and fear, chest pains started to develop. I thought that I had heart trouble, also, because I was brought back in thought to the family of my youth. My father died when I was twelve years of age of a massive coronary. I saw him fight for breath for thirty minutes or so. Since his death, my mother became afraid of dying with heart trouble. The doctors could never convince my mother that she did not have heart trouble. One of my brothers had an overproduction of blood and some of the others of eight children had symptoms of hypertension. So, with these thoughts of the past, I thought, "Surely I have heart trouble, because I feel the pain." Notice, thoughts grew into imaginations, and then to strongholds.

Finally, I went to the doctor to have tests run. At this time, my family physician was out of town practicing elsewhere, so I had to use another doctor who was well known in my town.

He ran an electrocardiogram and took blood samples as I requested. When I returned for the test results, he told me there was no sign of any disease or heart trouble. I refused to believe him. All he could do was give me some pills to take that might calm me down. My only trouble was that I *thought* I was sick.

Later my family physician moved back into town. As soon as he did, I went to him for identical tests, saying to myself, "Surely he will not lie to me, he will tell me straight." All results came back negative. "Now," I thought, "my own doctor has started lying to me." I would not believe him. The pains persisted. I would not accept anything but sickness—psychosomatic. But one day, I was riding in the back seat of the car as we were going to visit someone, trying to get them to church. I started thinking—"What in the world have I been doing?" I just settled it right there. I did not know anything about positive thinking at that time, but God blessed me. I said, "I will not worry about it any more. I will not die, I will not have heart trouble," and I continued saying that. The pain did not leave then. It kept coming but I found a Bible verse, Psalm 128:6, that says, "He that feareth the Lord shall see his children's children," and my children were small. I said, "I will take that for myself; I will receive that, so that gives me until the age of 40, at least." So I just started standing on the

Word of God. I started thinking like the Word taught, instead of thinking like I felt. You understand what I am talking about? Psychosomatics—that is how they get sick. They think themselves into sickness.

Remember now, I was a *born again* Christian for two years when this happened. It was not until eight years later that I heard the message of positive thinking; but God just directed me to start saying, "I will *LIVE* and not *DIE*." Soon the pains went away, the symptoms stopped. I am healthy now and have been since that day which was twelve years ago at this writing. There is nothing wrong with my body. That is the way you should think. You speak health to yourself and you will see later in these teachings that your words are going to produce. Right now we are talking about the mind. Your mind is going to control what you say.

We are going to let the peace of God rule in our hearts. I like what one teacher says. He says, "I am never confused. There is no confusion in the Word of God. I believe the Word of God over everything. So I am never confused. When the devil wants to confuse me, I just go to the Word of God, find the answer and I rely on the Word; therefore, I am not confused." I like that! I am never confused! So we will not be psychosomatic; we will be a "word-of-God-somatic!" WE are going to think health. That is only one area of your life, but this principle works in all areas.

5. Victory and Defeat Begin In The Mind

Let's look at a football team, for example. The coach gives them a pep talk before they go out. He is using *words* and *thoughts* to condition their minds to win, regardless of how large the players are on the opposing team. The team has purposed in their mind to carry the ball over the other goal, in spite of the opposition. They must think victory. If they think defeat, they will never win.

God's Word is *victory*. Start thinking God's Word in all situations. Victory or defeat is born in the mind.

Many of our heroes were down under, but they had it in their minds that no circumstance would stop them. They would say, "I do not care what it looks like, I am going out there." So remember that.

It does not matter what situation you are in, or what your capabilities are. If you can put correct thoughts in your mind, get that thought to become an imagination and become a stronghold, according to God's Word, then that Word will burn in your mind. It will come out of your mouth and you will direct your path according to the Word of God. This is the positive side of the thoughts, imaginations and strongholds.

6. Thoughts Are The Seeds Planted
In The Garden Of The Mind

Suppose that you plan to plant a garden one spring. After you prepare the soil and remove all rocks, trash and grass, you are ready to plant the seeds. Will you not take particular care to purchase seeds that are fresh, hybrid and exactly fit for your climate? You will also be careful to notice that you plant the correct seed according to the produce that you hope to harvest. You know that corn will produce corn, peas will produce peas and so on. As the garden progresses, although you did not plant weeds, some will come up with the vegetables. A good gardener will pull the weeds out so that the good plants will grow unhindered. So it is with your mind. Pull down the bad thoughts and only allow good thoughts to be planted in the garden of your mind, because everything that is left there will grow.

7. Exercise Your Will—Think Positive

You must start developing your will in this area. You start saying, "I will develop the habit of positive thinking." This is not just positive thinking. This is positive thinking in line with the Word of God. This is not *mind* over matter, but *mouth* over matter.

You can work for 12 hours a day without getting beat down and tired. Did you know that? You have done that, most probably. But at other times, you can work only two hours and you will be worn out. The difference is your attitude toward your job. You have experienced this and this is a way of thinking too. You have to relax and you have to know that you are in control, that you can perform your job. First of all, you have to like your job or accept your job the way you can enjoy it. It is the way you perform it and the way you are thinking in your mind, your attitude that will put you over. It is stress that is going to beat you. It matters not what job you are performing, if you stay under stress you will never make it.

A lady was telling me today that her husband comes out of his office holding his stomach because of pain. He cannot take it, the job is eating him up. He likes his job and he is trained for his job, but it has taken over him because of stress. The work is not doing it, but the stress is. I do not care what you are doing—you can do it if your mind is right.

There are some people who cannot do a thing. Is that right? Do you know some people like that? They just cannot do anything. Do you know why they cannot do anything? It is because they *think* they can do nothing. I had a Christian brother who could not do much. He would comment on it.

Personally, I always thought the opposite; I always thought I could do anything with my hands. But in the realm of studying in school or studying books or reading, I never thought I could do anything. Consequently, where did I apply myself? You know the answer.

Another brother has applied himself in the books and he knows the scripture. He can refer you to any part of the Bible any time he wants, but he has not done anything in mechanical areas because that is the way he has been thinking. Conversely, I always thought I could do anything I wanted to with wood. I could make anything I wanted. After I got older and saw what I had made, I saw that it was not very good work. But at the time I *thought* that it was the best. But then, ten years later, I looked back and saw that I was just learning then and had developed quite well in woodworking because I thought positively. If you think you can do it, you can develop in that area. Success is born in the mind. I would always say that if I could see someone do it, then I could do it too. I would just stay there long enough and learn something about it. Have you felt like that? You can train yourself in other areas. You must develop a habit to practice thought control.

Phil. 4:8 tells you what to think on — to fix your thoughts on those things that are true, that are honest, that are just and pure, lovely, of good report, virtue and of praise. That is a long list, isn't it? So every time I think now, I am going to have to go over this list.

8. Fear Will Prevent You From Speaking Faith

What are we talking about? Controlling the thoughts that come into your mind. You see, the scripture talks about it but we just have not been studying it. Sure, the average Christian just lets his mind wander anywhere it wants to and that is why it becomes trained in the wrong areas.

In our thinking there must be no fear. The Bible says "do not fear." Jesus says, "do not fear, do not worry." Matthew 6: "Do not have any anxieties, do not have any stress. Do not allow it in your thinking." You wonder how you can do that. You just do it. You might be lying in bed shaking with fear or you are nervous, but at that time you must begin to say, "I am not going to be nervous." You start thinking it. Say, "I will not worry, I will not be anxious." "I am going to sleep tonight." You start speaking that to yourself. Faith comes by hearing and hearing by the Word of God, Romans 10:17. Start speaking some of God's Word into yourself. II Timothy 1:7 says, "God has not given you a spirit of fear, but of love and power and a sound mind."

Fear will prevent you from speaking the correct things. Fear will cause you to be afraid that if you speak good things, Satan will combat you. You must realize that FEAR IS DEVIL FAITH. Faith is of God and produces life. Fear is of Satan and produces death. FEAR WILL ACTIVATE SATAN AS FAITH ACTIVATES GOD. John 10:10 says, "The thief cometh not but for to steal, and to kill, and to destroy: I am come that they might have life, and that they might have it more abundantly." Both fear and faith produce. You must realize that if you operate in fear, you will be producing misery and death in your life. Fear has torment. The Greek word, "phobos," that is translated, "fear," means: flight, dread, terror, to be intimidated by the enemy. But God's Word says, "We are the head, not the tail." I John 4:18 says, "Perfect love casteth out all fear."

Once, when my daughter was attacked by a physical malady, God showed me that I could not pray in *faith* until I was removed from *fear*. This was the setting.

After hearing the faith message, I decided to trust God for my health. My wife and three children agreed with me on this decision. Consequently, I canceled all of my health insurance.

Not many days hence, after the noon meal, my daughter of 14 years reported to me that she had been unable to urinate for three days due to some type of blockage. She also informed me that she was puffed and bloated and beginning to be in pain.

The immediate response was *FEAR*. It grabs you in the pit of your stomach. There is a rise of breath—suspense.

My wife and I looked into each other's face without speaking for a few moments. Our thoughts were the same. The question was, what are we going to say and do?

First, my wife spoke, half statement, half question. "You'd better take her to the doctor."

I said, "Wait a minute now."

Both of us still having the same thoughts, she replied, "But this is *serious*."

I said, "I *know* this is serious, but we decided that God would meet our healing needs."

FEAR . . . FEAR . . . FEAR!!!

The Spirit of God interrupted, "Get rid of FEAR."

We agreed together and commanded the spirit of fear to leave us completely.

Then I called our pastor and he came over, agreed with us in prayer, as I cursed the spirit that was attacking my daughter's body and commanded it to leave.

It was then 2 p.m., time for me to leave for work. All afternoon I had to keep the Bible handy, because fear continued to attack my mind. Every time my mind would start to fear, I would read scripture to drive away fear. I could not afford to fear.

When I returned home from work, about 11:30 p.m., I questioned my wife, and spoke to my daughter, learning that she was completely healed and comfortable, having been able to use the rest-room three times in that 8 hour period. Thanks be to Jesus.

I said all of that to say this. "We cannot allow our minds to stay in fear, for if we do, we will not allow ourselves to pray the prayer of faith." When you prepare to pray, do not pray in fear, pray in faith. God does not honor fear. He honors faith. Submit everything to God in love and resist the devil.

9. You Must Know God's Will For Your Life

You have to know God's will for your life in order for you to think correctly. This is where many people are tripped up, because they do not know God's will for their lives. If you do not know where you are going, how can you apply faith and correct words to direct your life?

In order to hit a target at 300 yards, you have to use a rifle and not a scatter gun. In the same way you must rifle your faith to direct all its energy toward the target of your life. If you do not know where the target is or you do not know what you are aiming at, how can you direct the shot? Now, apply this to your own life and ask yourself, "What am I aiming at? Toward what point am I directing my life? Do I know God's will for my life?'' If you do not know the answers to these questions, then pay particular attention to the next few paragraphs.

God does not have to show you your whole future—I doubt that He will—but God is willing to give you the next step that He wants you to make.

My own confession is that for many years after salvation, I served in the church, doing good things, tithing, etc. . . . . . . One day, I saw what I needed to do. Mark 11:24 says, ''Whatsoever things you desire, when you pray, believe that ye receive them, and ye shall have them.'' I said, ''Father, I *desire* to know your will for my life. According to Mark 11:24, I ask you for it, I receive it, and thank you for it.'' Then the confession of my mouth was that I knew God's will for my life by faith.

Soon, God instructed me to resign public work. There was the directive will. But what should I do after I quit my job? The answer came, ''I will give you further directions as you execute the directions you have.'' God is still directing my life one step at a time. You must find out the next step in your life, so that you can speak it into existence. Start thinking according to God's directions for your life. Remember, as a man thinks in his heart, *so is he*.

Chapter II

The Abundance of the Heart

We said in the last chapter, "As a man thinks in his heart, so is he." We will now see how the heart controls the mouth. We are going to start in Matthew 12:34-37. Now we are looking unto our teacher, Jesus, because we are reading the words of Jesus as He was teaching this to the Pharisees. We will see what Jesus thought about the words of your mouth. Matthew 12:34 says, "Oh generation of vipers, how can you, being evil, speak good things?" They were trying to put forth a false front, you see. Jesus said, "Wait a minute, you cannot speak good things, for out of the abundance of the heart, the mouth speaks." Is Jesus speaking to us? He says, do not try to cover up. What is in your heart is going to come out of your mouth. You might cover it up for a while, but just as soon as you get aggravated or you get the opportunity, it is coming out of your mouth, from your heart. It is said that when a man gets drunk, he starts to tell on himself, because he starts acting like he really is. He lets go. Jesus says that your mouth is telling what is in your heart. He says that a *good* man, out of the *good* treasure of his heart (verse 35), bringeth forth *good* things. It is kind of a chain reaction. He says that the *evil* man, out of the *evil* treasures of his heart, bringeth forth *evil* things: "but I say unto you that every idle word that men shall speak, they shall give account of in the day of judgment."

Then in verse 37 He says, "For by your words you will be justified, and by your words you will be condemned." Now, if you want to see how true that is, just get arrested. The arresting officer has to state your rights to you. What are your rights? The right to remain silent. Why? If you do not remain silent, whatever you say can be held against you. You can *hang* yourself by talking. The officer has to tell you to keep your mouth shut. If you do say anything, he is going to use it against you. This is a warning.

In the spiritual world, the devil is the "*slick lawyer*" that is trying to *hang* you with your words. He will use your words to accuse you to the Father. Rev. 12:10 calls Satan the accuser of the brethren. This word for accuser is *KATEGOREO,* to accuse in judicial procedure. The usual word for the devil is *diaballo,* to slander, but this word is not used here. Also, in Job 1:9-11, the devil accuses Job before the Father.

We cannot afford to give the accuser any words to use against us. We have to give our lawyer, Jesus, good FAITH-filled words to use in our plea before the Father.

Now, of course, we know that the Jews, before they would eat anything, would be careful to wash their hands, cups and dishes and kill all the germs, because they did not want to defile the body. But Jesus came with a new ruling here. He said, in Matthew 15:11, "not that which goeth into the mouth of the man but that which cometh out of the mouth defileth a man." The Jews were looking at the physical law. Jesus was telling them of the spiritual law. He said, "It is not going to hurt you to eat something with germs on it, because your body is equipped to get rid of that, and there is no problem." Of course, even the disciples could not understand it. They said, "Wait a minute, Master, before you get away, why don't you explain this to us?"

In verse 17 Jesus said, "Don't you understand that whatsoever entereth in at the mouth goeth into the belly and is cast out into the draught, but those things which proceed out of the mouth, come forth from the heart and they defile a man."

It is your *words* that are producing. "For out of the heart proceed evil thoughts, murders, adulteries, fornications, thefts, false witnesses, blasphemies; these are the things that defile a man. But to eat with unwashed hands defileth not a man," it is only physical. Your heart is the real you. Jesus is presenting a simple teaching here: that your words will tell what you are and either condemn you or justify you. Your words are an extension of yourself. The real you is your spirit—is that right? Your words are spirit and they are an extension of you. When you put out words, they are a part of you and you are responsible for them. Nobody else is responsible except you. Jesus is talking about the heart—not only the words. You may say, "I said that, but I did not mean it. Oh, I am sorry, I did not mean to hurt your feelings." That is not true. You said it because that is what came out of your heart. That is what you felt in your innermost being. That is why you said it and later on you want to excuse yourself. That is no excuse. You might apologize for gossiping, but that does not dull the effects of your words. It is like getting a feather pillow and making a hole in it and going down the street scattering feathers all over. Now, after you do that, try to pick up all the feathers and put them back in the pillow. That would be hard to do. That is how your words are. After they go out, you cannot call them back. It is better to just keep them in. Bite your lip.

Proverbs 16:23 has something to say about this. "The heart of the wise teacheth his mouth, and addeth learning to his lips." You see, your heart can be good for you, if your heart is wise. How does your heart get wisdom? From the Word of God. You pour the Word of God into you, then the heart of the wise is going to teach understanding to your mouth and learning to your lips.

1. Keep Guard on Your Heart

Proverbs 4:20—5:2—This is God's Word saying, why don't you learn my ways? Proverbs 4:20—"My son, attend to my words, incline thine ear to my sayings." Now, if you want to know how to change your heart, this is it right here. He says, "incline your ear to my sayings, let them not depart from thine eyes, keep them in the midst of your heart." Where do you keep them? In the middle of your heart, in your spirit. You take the Words of God and put them in your heart, "for they are life unto those that find them and health to all their flesh. Keep your heart with all diligence for out of it are the issues of life." You see, the Bible is backing itself up. Where are your words coming from? Out of the heart are the issues of life. How do you put the issues of life out? With your *mouth* you put out the issues of life.

Verse 24—"Put away from thee a froward mouth." You see, He is showing you how to control your life. Put the Word of God into your heart because this is where your life is coming from. "Put away from thee a froward mouth and perverse lips put far from thee." You see what the Bible is saying? "Let thine eyelids look straight before thee. Ponder the path of thy feet and let all thy ways be established." How do you establish your ways? With your *mouth* — let all your ways be established with your mouth. "Turn not to the right nor to the left, remove thy foot from evil. My son, attend to my wisdom and bow thine ear to my understanding." Look at the next verse — "that thou mayest regard discretion and that thy lips may keep knowledge." Over and over again, the Bible talks about this. Here the Bible is saying to keep your heart by the Word of God. Feed your heart, because as you feed your heart, you will see your language changing. You will still be speaking English, but you will be speaking life instead of death.

One fellow says to read the Bible just as you do the newspaper. How do you read the newspaper? You see the price of meat going up. It is going to double next week. What do you do? You go out and buy a lot of meat before it goes up. Is that right? You read the newspaper and you act upon it as it is going to affect you. Well, read the Bible the same way, like it is going to affect you. The Bible says keep your mouth shut. What are you going to do? "O.K.," do you promise? Eccl. 5:2—Let your words be *few*.

A well-known world evangelist gave the following testimony and this is what changed his ministry. For seven years he was preaching full time. He did not have much of a ministry but still preached his heart out. He said, "Something is wrong here, something is not producing, so I am going to have to try something." Then he got the bright idea. "I know what I will do. I will go to the Bible and start reading it as if I have never read it before, as if this is the first time I have ever read it and every word I am going to take literally." He had preached seven years with no results. The eighth year he started getting results because he started taking the Bible literally. He started believing what it said and he now has a world-renowned ministry that is second to none. If you are not fully grounded in God's financial prosperity plan, do not visit his museum. That is right. He could live for the rest of his life just on his museum. It is just too big for the carnal mind. But you know how he started? He said, "I am going to read the Word of God like it is true, as if God meant what He said." *God's Word in this man's heart did it.* Let's take the Word of God just as it is and apply it to what we are going to do with our mouth. It will change your life completely.

Proverbs 17:7 says, "Excellent speech becometh not a fool." Did you ever see a fool talking wisely? But he says, "much less do lying lips a prince." If you know a prince, you do not expect him to lie to you.

Proverbs 17:28—"Even a fool when he holdeth

his peace is counted wise, and he that shutteth his lips is esteemed a man of understanding.'' Your mouth will betray you or show forth your heart. If you do not speak, many people will think that you are wise. Often people get the wrong idea that they have to talk to be important or counted wise. The Bible teaches us the opposite. We have used this chapter to see that our words are proceeding from our heart. This is really *over-simplified*. There is more that we must take into consideration; such as, the *renewed mind* and the part it plays with your spirit and heart.

Next, we will examine man's construction or ''*makeup*.''

Chapter III

These Things
Ought Not to Be

We will consider again the teaching of Jesus in Matt. 12:34-37, where He is teaching on *words*. Here we are studying the *PRODUCTION* of words.

In verse 34 He asked, "How can you, being evil, speak good things? Because out of the abundance of the heart the mouth speaks." He continues in verse 35 saying that our words will be composed or manufactured from the storage of either good or bad treasure that is within us. Also, in Luke 6:43-45 He compares us to a tree: "Make the tree good and the fruit good or the tree bad and the fruit bad."

So, Jesus seems to be saying, if you are "*good*" then your words will be "*good*." If you are "*bad*" your words will be "*bad*."

We need some revelation truth to understand fully what the lesson is to be here. In James chapter 3, James is teaching on the tongue. He asks in vs. 12, "Can a fig tree bear olives? A vine, figs? Can a fountain send forth both *salt* and *fresh* water?"

These things *ought not* to be," he says in vs. 10—"OUGHT NOT TO BE."

Evidently they were in existence. What was it that "ought not to be?" Verse 9—"Therewith we bless God, and curse men." If the man is good, he should put out good words—if he is bad, he should put out bad words. Again, what is the problem here? The same mouth is putting forth both good and bad words. This *ought not* to be.

So, we can conclude that a good man does not "always" put out good words. Why is this true? The answer lies in the understanding of the makeup of man. The mouth, at one moment, will be controlled by the abundance of the heart, and the next moment, controlled by the unstable emotions and the mind—producing salt and fresh water from the same fountain.

At this point, we will engage in a short study of the components of man, considering mainly the following four words: HEART, SPIRIT, SOUL, BODY.

In I Thess. 5:23, the Bible uses three of these words in describing man, but does not use the word "heart." We find here the following words:

(GREEK)   (ENGLISH)
PNEUMA = SPIRIT— Air or wind
PSUCHE = SOUL —Mind, will, emotion
SOMA   = BODY — Physical flesh

Here, the word "heart" is *not* used but is used in

other places to refer to the central part of the entire man. The Greek word for heart is *"KARDIA"* which is translated *heart,* or *bowels* and can refer to *belly, inner man, hidden man,* depending on the translation you are reading.

Now, the question we are concerned with is this: What exactly does the heart include? Is it only the spirit; is it the spirit and soul; or all three, spirit, soul and body?

For the benefit of understanding this study, let us use the following definition. We will combine the spirit, soul, and body, thus having a sum total of the whole man; and then say that the heart is the *"center"* of the *entire mental and moral activity* of the *"complete person."*

Now, we still have the original statement, "Out of the abundance of the heart, the mouth speaks." Good heart—good words, bad heart—bad words.

When is the heart good or bad? It must be a combination of all three:

1. A regenerated Spirit.
2. A renewed Mind.
3. A living sacrificed Body (Rom. 12:1-2).

One without the other two is not complete, neither is two without the other one. For this reason Romans 12:1-2 deals with the body and mind. The spirit, at this point, is regenerated; but the body has to be given as a living sacrifice to be controlled by the direction of the Holy Spirit and the mind has to be conformed to the Word of God so that it can cooperate with what God is doing. Therefore, we conclude this following chain of command.

God speaks to man by His Holy Spirit to man's recreated human spirit; in turn the human spirit directs the soul (MIND, WILL, EMOTIONS) of the man and then the mind directs the body, including the tongue; thus, the whole man, walking and talking like a son of GOD.

Just as the chain of command works in an Army, so should the chain of command operate in a believer's total person. The Army moves coordinated as the *private* takes orders from the *sergeant*, and so on up the line to the *commander-in-chief*.

As man gets his tongue, mind, will, emotions, soul, body, and spirit trained to take orders from the Holy Spirit, he begins to speak correctly according to the Word of God.

The good tree will produce good fruit. James 1:26 tells us that a religious man's *mouth* can "fool" his own *heart*.

Anytime someone confesses words that are not agreeable with scripture, that person's mouth is fooling his own self. The reason is this: If the person's spirit is regenerated and has God's Holy Spirit living within, the Holy Spirit will only direct words that agree with the Holy *WORD*. So, if that person speaks contrary to the *WORD*, then he is naturally speaking against the Holy Spirit that is within his own heart.

Then we understand that the words proceeding from us should be directed in a way that they will agree with God's Word at all times.

As we get our complete *heart* obeying God's directions, we will produce God-directed words.

Chapter IV

Salvation is Based on Right Confession of Jesus

Rom. 10:8, "The *WORD OF FAITH* is near thee, in thy *mouth* and in thy *heart.*"

But we must *speak* that word. "That if thou shalt *confess with thy mouth* the Lord Jesus, and shalt believe in thine *heart* that God has raised Him from the dead, thou shalt be saved. For with the *heart* (center of complete being) man believes unto righteousness and with the *mouth confession is made unto salvation.*"

Verse 13 says, "For whosoever shall *call* upon the name of the Lord *shall* be saved."

You will not *confess* Jesus unless you *believe* Jesus. But how can you believe if you haven't *heard?* (Faith comes by hearing, Rom. 10:17). You must hear before you can believe. HEAR WHAT? The "WORD" from God. But how can they hear without a preacher? What does a preacher's job consist of but *speaking* the Word of God?

Notice, the words used in the above sentences—WORDS, MOUTH, SPEAK, CON-

FESS, CALL, BELIEVE, HEART, HEARD, WORDS, PREACH, WORDS—AND THE WORD IS JESUS.

The most important issue in your life is based upon your confession and belief of Jesus.

In Matthew 10:32-33, Jesus makes another profound statement about confession. "Confess me before men, and I'll confess you before the Father, and if you deny me, I'll deny you."

Let us get hold of the real meaning of this scripture and not pass it off as another statement *limited to salvation,* as natural man thinks about salvation.

Looking at the real extract of the word used here, we see the Greek word *"homologeo." Homos* means *same* and *lego* means *to speak.* The whole word means to speak the same as and to agree—to agree with what?

This *homologeo* has an "en" with it followed by a personal pronoun. In other words, this means to confess in a name, the nature of the confession being determined by the *context* of the confession, always in agreement with what Jesus (the Word) says.

Whatever we confess in the name of Jesus that agrees with what He says, He will confess for us before the Father, and Jesus cannot confess it for us if we do not confess it for ourselves. If we deny Him, He will deny us; for really, if we deny Him, we deny ourselves.

This means more that just stepping into salvation. It means the whole of life. It engulfs everything that the WORD says. This is the "POWER of ATTORNEY" of JESUS' NAME.

This is how we obtain the great and precious promises: prosperity, health, deliverance, rest, peace of mind, victory and authority over Satan. Jesus already has obtained the victory. We only have to confess it for ourselves, agree with Him, that I *am* an overcomer, more than a conqueror, a wonder unto many, can do all things, have all things, et cetera, et cetera, et cetera! Whatever the WORD says, I say in Jesus' Name—and then He says it for me before the Father—Hallelujah!

Therefore, (Heb. 10:23) "Let us hold fast to the profession (confession) of our faith, without wavering."

So then we must confess Jesus as Lord and Savior to receive salvation and then confess what is ours unto possession.

"Positionally" all things *are* ours, but to bring them into manifestation, we must confess them into the physical world. *"Legally"* we have our complete inheritance as joint-heirs with Jesus in the spiritual realm and we come to possess this inheritance in the physical realm by speaking them into being.

For example, just as your salvation was wrought on the cross 2,000 years ago, you didn't *receive* it until you *confessed* it. So, also, our complete inheritance was paid for and obtained 2,000 years ago, but we only receive it as we confess it. This understanding opens unto us a greater revelation of Hebrews 3:1 which we will consider in the next chapter.

Chapter V

Jesus Placed Himself at the Service of Our Words

Heb. 3:1 — "Consider *Jesus* the *Apostle* and *High Priest* of our confession."

This chapter compares Jesus and Moses. Moses was faithful as a "go-between" for God and His people. But at times Moses cried unto God and said the people wearied him with their murmurings, complaining, and lack of faith.

But now Jesus is our "go-between." Do we weary Jesus with our complaining and speaking words of doubt?

Notice that Hebrews 3:1 calls Jesus the *Apostle* and *High Priest* of our confession. In other words, He is considering *what we say* when He approaches the Father on our behalf. Jesus is our mediator and representative with the Father.

Let's now look at the words, "Apostle" and "High Priest" in this verse. An apostle is one that is *sent* or "one sent forth."

The noun, "apostolos," comes from the verb "apostello," which is the act of sending forth someone on a mission to do something in behalf of the sender.

For instance, if I sent you to the bank to get some money out of my account, I would have to give you a check with my signature as a necessary credential.

An ambassador of a country speaks in behalf of the country he represents.

Jesus came as an Apostle of God to us. He finished that work. Now, He has placed Himself as *our* Apostle to the Father. He represents us to the Father. He is the *Apostle of our confession*, the Apostle of *what we say*. Jesus is *sent forth* by what we say. (Reread this paragraph and realize the heaviness of Heb. 3:1.)

When we confess Jesus as Lord, Jesus confesses our salvation before the Father. When we say, "I am healed by the stripes of Jesus," then Jesus can say that I am healed by His stripes. If I confess that I am sick Jesus cannot use that confession, but the devil can use it to accuse me to the Father.

So, let's give Jesus some FAITH-filled words to use on our behalf.

Jesus is also the *High Priest* of our confession. The priest always offered up only what was brought to him by the people.

Jesus provided His blood as the eternal complete sacrifice for our sins, but the Bible tells us to offer the *Sacrifice of Praise*.

Jesus, our High Priest, can only represent us to

the Father to the extent that we allow Him to.

Give Him a good sacrifice of PRAISE.

Give Him a good confession of FAITH.

He is ready and willing to confess us before the Father in Heaven.

Chapter VI

The Power and Importance of Words

Genesis, chapter 1, shows us that God created with words—Let there be . . . and it was.

Jeremiah 5:22—''Fear ye not me? saith the Lord: will ye not tremble at my presence, which have placed the sand for the bound of the sea by a perpetual decree, that it cannot pass it: and though the waves thereof toss themselves, yet can they not prevail; though they roar, yet can they not pass over it?''

The sea has to stay within the boundary of the sand because of a perpetual decree by God. This is also supported by Ps. 104:9.

The tidal wave may come but it has to return into the sea. The tide comes in but it *must* return. The devil may attack you with his roar or sickness and other waves of attacks, but they cannot stay, they *must* return. The reason why they must return is because you may decree the boundary of the devil. Job 22:28 says, ''Thou shalt also decree a thing and it shall be established unto thee, and light shall shine upon thy ways.'' Have you made any decrees? What have you been decreeing? Have you been making a decree of fear, sickness, etc., or do you decree 120 years of complete health, strength and youth as was afforded to Moses?

Be very careful of what you say *because it shall be established* for you. Speak your future, direct your paths by speaking the Word of God.

Proverbs 18:21—"Death and life are in the power of the tongue." We can speak *life* for ourselves and others or we can speak *death* to ourselves and others. We not only CAN but WE DO.

Numbers 35:30 says that the murderer will be put to death by the *mouth of witnesses*. If the witness will not speak, the judge cannot hang the murderer.

Mark 11:14—Jesus spoke to the fig tree and it died. He spoke death to the tree. In Mark 11:23 Jesus said, if *You* will say it, you will have it. Speak *TO* the mountain—speak *TO*, speak *TO* . . . . There is power in words. "He shall have whatsoever He saith."

Chapter VII

God Had to Shut the Mouths of Some People

Sometimes God had a plan to fill and could not let people talk to hinder the working of the plan.

We see this in Joshua 6:10 as instructions were given to ruin the walls of Jericho. The men were instructed not to make any sound with their mouth until the seventh day on the seventh round when they were to shout. They could not speak a word.

Why could they not be trusted? The reason is that they would have murmured, complained and spoken doubt. They would have talked themselves out of a victory.

In Luke 1:18-20 we see that Zacharias could not be trusted to speak because he did not believe that his wife could give birth to John the Baptist. The angel Gabriel told Zacharias that the words that he spoke were words to be fulfilled. It was a plan of God, and because of his unbelief he could not be trusted to speak. But in verses 60-64, we see that after Zacharias wrote on a paper that his name would be John, he could speak again. He could then be trusted to speak.

Mary, on the other hand, said, "Be it unto me according to Thy Word," and she pondered these things in her heart and she did not go up and down the neighborhood telling all that she knew. God could trust her with the birth of Jesus.

We see also, that Jesus had to keep his mouth shut to bring to pass the plan of God for his crucifixion.

Acts 8:32, "Like a Lamb, dumb before His shearers, He opened not His mouth." *DUMB* means *SILENT*.

In Matthew 26:62-66, "And the high priest arose, and said unto him, Answerest thou nothing? What is it which these witness against thee? But Jesus held his peace. And the high priest answered and said unto him, I adjure thee by the living God, that thou tell us whether thou be the Christ, the Son of God. Jesus saith unto him, Thou hast said: neverthless I say unto you, Hereafter shall ye see the Son of man sitting on the right hand of power, and coming in the clouds of heaven. Then the high priest rent his clothes, saying, He hath spoken blasphemy; what further need have we of witnesses? Behold, now ye have heard his blasphemy. What think ye? They answered and said, He is guilty of death."

Jesus was silent at His trial before the high priest. He said just enough to HANG HIMSELF (verse 64).

In Matthew 27:11-14, "And Jesus stood before the governor and the governor asked him, saying, Art thou the King of the Jews? And Jesus said unto him, Thou sayest. And when he was accused of the chief priests and elders, he answered *nothing*. Then said Pilate unto him, Hearest thou not how many things they witness against thee? And he answered him to *never a word;* insomuch that the governor marvelled greatly."

Before Pilate, Jesus did not say anything. He was very careful.

We remember that Moses asked God, "Who shall I say sent me?" God said, "Tell them the *I AM* sent you." Then at the arrest of Jesus, the soldiers asked if that was he that they should take, Jesus answered, "I AM." At the pronouncement of that name, "I AM" the soldiers fell backwards under the power of that spoken name (John 18:5-6).

At the trial, Jesus could not speak even His name because it would have freed Him. He HAD to remain silent. Pilate tried to get Him to talk so that he could release Him, but Jesus would not speak. He came to give Himself as a lamb.

We can learn a lesson here. We should only speak those things that we want people to KNOW. Also, in your spiritual conflict with the enemy, don't tell him everything. Don't tell him where you are hurting. This is like a spy seeking top secret information of the enemy country in order to defeat them. So, do not tell the devil what is going on. He will not know unless you tell him. Satan cannot read your mind, unless you deal in ESP or telepathy. We see this in scripture as the devil was trying to kill Jesus as a young boy. Herod sent the three wise men to find Jesus, but the angel told them to go to their own country. Herod then began to kill all the boy babies under two years of age and the angel told Joseph to take Jesus into Egypt. Satan *did not know that* Jesus was in Egypt, or else he would have sought Him out there to kill Him. You see, no one *told* Satan *who* the Savior was and no one told him *where* he was. Satan could not find Jesus to kill him.

The Bible says that we are *hid* in Christ and the devil cannot find us, so he goes about roaring like a lion trying to get us to come out (say something) so that he can tell where we are. But if you do not *tell* Satan what is going on, he will not know. Tell him what you want him to know, such as, "Jesus is Lord," "I've got power," "I'm an overcomer," "I'm more than a conqueror," "I'm healed, saved and delivered out of darkness."

So, we see that the first time that the devil could level his attacks at Jesus was after the public announcement at the baptism, "This is my Beloved Son." Then Satan followed Jesus into the wilderness and began to tempt Him.

We should not suspect that Satan knows everything, because he does not.

God's ways are *spiritually* discerned and Satan does not receive the things of God. If he could, he would have understood the prophecy of Elizabeth to Mary and the prophecy of Simeon and Anna in the temple over the baby Jesus in Luke 2:25-38.

But he did not understand or perceive God's plan of the Savior. He knew that God was doing something but couldn't put his finger on it.

So, do not fear Satan knowing your thoughts or plans, just tell him what he needs to know. You are in control with the correct use of your tongue. DO NOT BE HUNG BY YOUR TONGUE!

Chapter VIII

The Tongue
Controls Your Life

Just as you confess salvation, you can confess health, riches, freedom, safety and whatever else the scripture promises you.

Prov. 21:23, "Whoso keepeth his mouth and his tongue keepeth his soul from troubles."

Prov. 12:25, "Heaviness in the heart of man maketh it stoop: but a good word maketh it glad."

I HATE YOU!! I LOVE YOU!!

These are only words, but they are powerful words. Which ones do you like to hear spoken to you? What effect do they have on you? Think about it.

Sometimes you are very careful about what you speak. For instance, you go to a funeral parlor to pay last respects to a friend and to greet his family. On your way to the meeting of the loved ones, you begin to think, "What shall I say to the family to encourage them?" You surely do not want to hurt them at a time like this. You become very careful about *what you say*.

Why should we be on guard only at a funeral

parlor? Let's be careful to minister grace to the hearers all of the time.

Prov. 10:19-20, "In the multitude of words there wanteth not sin: but he that refraineth his lips is wise. The tongue of the just is as choice silver: the heart of the wicked is little worth."

Many of the scriptures that I am quoting in these pages need no comment but just adherence.

Prov. 12:18, "The *tongue* of the *wise* is *health.*"

In I Sam. 3:19, God guards our words if they are correct. "And Samuel grew, and the Lord was with him and did not let any of his words fall to the ground."

Prov. 12:6, "The mouth of the upright shall deliver him."

Prov. 18:6-8, "A fool's lips enter into contention, and his mouth calleth for strokes. A fool's mouth is his destruction, and his lips are the snare of his soul. The words of a talebearer are as wounds, and they go down into the innermost parts of the belly."

Has your mouth ever gotten you into a fight? "The mouth calls for strokes."

As often as I teach this message, I ask the hearers to do some homework, and it is this: open your own Bible to Proverbs and read through it verse by verse, meditating on each verse. Have a colored pencil in your hand and color every verse that deals with the mouth, tongue or words. You will be richly rewarded.

Also, go to James and read chapter three. James said not to be many teachers because teachers will receive the greater condemnation. Why? There are four reasons, at least:

1. *Words* are the teacher's main *tool*.
2. His *words* are *many*, good chance to offend.
3. He speaks to more *ears* than others do.
4. Because of his position, some people will take his words and live by them.

And then James goes on to liken the tongue to a rudder on a ship. The rudder controls the direction of the ship, your tongue controls the direction of your life.

Also, consider the small BIT in the horse's mouth.

God has used much of the Bible to teach us about the importance of words.

Chapter IX

The Tongue Brings
Increase or Decrease

Prov. 18:20, "A man's belly shall be satisfied with the fruit of his mouth; and with the increase of his lips shall he be filled."

Prov. 13:2-3, "A man shall eat good by the fruit of his mouth: but the soul of the transgressors shall eat violence. He that keepeth his mouth keepeth his life: but he that openeth wide his lips shall have destruction."

One Bible teacher testifies that after a teaching, an old man in his nineties came up and gave him the following testimony. Said the old gentleman, "You can see that I have a full head of black hair and at my age this is rarely seen. Well, God showed me a long time ago how I could keep my hair. Also, I have a perfect set of teeth at this old age; plus, I still have 20-20 vision and my eye is not dim. God showed me at an early age how to keep these things. But the FIRST thing that God showed me how to keep was my *TONGUE*, and in keeping my tongue, I could keep the rest of these things."

Do not allow yourself to talk yourself out of hair,

teeth and sight. Also, concerning your vigor, strength, vitality and youth, quote Ps. 105 which says, "The Lord satisfies my *mouth* with good things *so that* my youth is renewed like the eagle's."

Also, Isa. 40:31, "They that wait upon the Lord shall renew their strength, they shall mount up with wings as eagles, they shall run and not be weary and they shall walk and not faint."

Do not ever confess, "I'm tired." What good will that do you? If you feel tired, just say, "my strength is renewed as the eagles." Enter into some rest and relaxation and cause yourself to rest. This will overcome the tiredness, but do not continue to confess that you are BUSHED.

Do not *"POOR MOUTH."* Remember, a man shall be satisfied with the fruit of his mouth; so *"RICH MOUTH"* instead.

Prov. 12:13-14, "The wicked is snared by the transgression of his lips: but the just shall come out of trouble. A man shall be satisfied with good by the fruit of his mouth: and the recompence of a man's hands shall be rendered unto him."

Prov. 16:21-24, "The *sweetness* of the lips increase learning—the heart of the wise teaches his *mouth* and adds learning to his *lips*. Pleasant *words* are as an honeycomb, sweet to the soul and *health* to the bones."

Ps. 101:5, "Whoso privily slandereth his

neighbour, him will I cut off: him that hath an high look and a proud heart will not I suffer.''

Prov. 18:8, ''The words of a talebearer are as wounds, and they go down into the innermost parts of the belly.''

Chapter X

We Become God-Possessed

This is the opposite of demon possession. We speak God's Word, and agree with God. We lend our members unto Him and His servants we are.

"Speaking to yourselves in psalms and hymns and spiritual songs, singing and making melody in your hearts to the Lord" (Eph. 5:19).

"Let the word of Christ dwell in you richly in all wisdom, teaching and admonishing one another in psalms and hymns and spiritual songs, singing with grace in your hearts to the Lord" (Col. 3:16).

Preach the *WORD* (II Tim. 4:2). Speak the truth in love (Eph. 4:15).

1. Make A Decision

We must make a *DECISION*. We will do nothing without a decision. Say this for yourself. "I am purposed in my heart that my mouth shall not transgress" (Ps. 17:3).

Also, Eccl. 5:6, "Suffer not (permit not) your mouth to cause your flesh to sin."

Paul warned Timothy in II Tim. 2 not to strive about *words* of no value. They will subvert the hearers, and cause the new converts to fall. He was referring to doctrines instead of God's Word. Let us avoid foolish questions, refrain our tongue from evil and our lips that they speak no guile, speaking evil of no man.

2. Jesting

Eph. 5:4 prohibits jesting and foolish and silly talking along with fornication, uncleanness, and filthiness.

Jesting is the main word we want to understand here. We should be very concerned about jesting. It means a statement that can be easily turned to mean something else, to adapt to moods and conditions of those it is dealing with at the time. Jesting can HURT very much. Like complimenting someone publicly on a point that everyone knows that they are especially weak on. It could be calling a fat sister by the name of "SLIM" or a bald brother by the name of "CURLY."

Jesting is: polished and witty speech; an instrument of sin; refined versatility without Christian flavor or grace; lodged in a sly question; a smart answer; a hint; an insinuation; sarcasm; exaggeration; figurative expression; acute nonsense; unaccountable and inexplicable—but answerable in numberless rovings; fancy windings of language convenient at the moment *regardless* of being *exactly true.*

Matt. 5:37 says, "Let your yea be yea and your nay be nay, whatever is more than this comes from evil."

Eccl. 5:2, "Let thy words be *FEW*." Does that speak to you? Anyway, who ever said that much talking made you important? Who wants to hear you talk all of the time? What is wrong with silence? Conquer silence and then come out speaking God's word, speaking life and victory in Jesus. Our YES will mean YES; our NO will mean NO. When you hear me speak, you may hold me responsible because I've said what I meant and mean what I say. I refuse to be *HUNG BY MY TONGUE!*

Chapter XI

We are the Ministers of Life, Not Death

We are builders, not killers. Since we know that our words are creative, we should be careful of what we create. We can create life or death.

I was called to a home to minister to a man that is not a converted man. He was highly nervous and did not know what direction to take in his life. When I arrived, I realized he was not particularly interested in being preached to. Therefore, we just sat down and entered into conversation. I purposed to speak life to him. I do not recall exactly what I said except that I gave him only positive reports of what God had done in our life and what God was doing today in the earth. The result was that he could get back on his feet, make some good decisions and take hold of his life.

You, my brother, can speak life to someone today. Refuse to do otherwise. Refrain from speaking death, discouragement, and despair to anyone. I *exhort* you to experiment today. Speak life and watch for the results.

"Let your speech be always with grace, seasoned with salt, that ye may know how ye ought to answer every man'' (Col. 4:6).

"Let no corrupt communication proceed out of your mouth, but that which is good, to the use of edifying, that it may minister grace to the *HEARER*" (Eph. 4:29). Keep in mind the hearer and the effect upon them.

When I was a young boy about the age of 13 or 14, I was working with other young boys in a grocery store. On one particular morning, I asked one of the other boys how he was feeling. He said that he felt well and everything was chipper. I replied that he did not look well and that he may be a little pale. He looked all right but I thought I would just play a little joke on him. (This was a dreadful thing to do and I'll not do it again, of course, for I've received forgiveness from God.) Nevertheless, I persuaded the other boys to participate with me in the "gag." In rotation, we would each take a turn telling this one fellow that he looked pale or asking, ''Are you *sure* you feel all right?'' After a full morning of this he was feeling quite bad, and by lunch time he went home sick. He told the boss that he had to go home and go to bed due to the fact that he had become sick. It's a sick trick, I'll agree, but it tells one what the Bible says, "Life and death are in the power of the tongue.''

So, therefore, I will speak of those things that

are honest, just, pure, lovely, of good report, that have virtue and praise (Phil. 4:8).

Jesus said in Mark 4:24 to be careful of what you *HEAR* also, because, "what you hear" will be multiplied unto you. Hear the words of life and receive life multiplied; hear the world and you have zero. Anything multiplied by zero equals zero. So, as we consider "words," they have power when you *speak* them and they have power when you *hear* them. FAITH comes by hearing. The right kind of faith comes by hearing the Word of God (Rom. 10:17).

Have you known of someone who was a habitual storyteller? He told untrue stories all the time. In fact, you could not depend on anything that he said. After a period of time he, being well-known in the community, would gain the reputation of being the one that "lies so much that he now believes his own lies."

Words produce FAITH—either good or bad, depending on the words.

If we continue to quote scripture from God's Holy Word, then we will be hearing, and hearing the Word of God, ever building our faith to the point that we believe every *Word* of God.

Chapter XII

David and the Giant

In the Bible account of David and the giant in I Sam. 17, we see a good lesson dealing with the words of your mouth and the content of your heart.

The two armies were facing each other on the side of two mountains with a valley in between. Israel on one side and the Philistines on the other.

Every day there was the giant that would come out into the valley and speak to the Israelites. The Bible calls this man the *champion of the Philistines*. He was 9 feet 9 inches tall, had a helmet of brass, a coat which was made with brass shingles weighing about 155 pounds, a spear which weighed about 19 pounds, and he had a man to hold his shield before him. He was quite a large man to have to face. Remember that many problems that you might have to face will come dressed as giants, but we are learning what to do with giants.

We see in I Sam. 17:8-11 that the giant, Goliath, would come out every day and speak *words*. He was able to put fear into the armies of God with these words. (This reminds me of a famous BOXER who would prepare his opposing fighter with a profusion of *words*.)

Goliath would say, "Give me a man to fight. If he wins, we will be your servants, and if I win you will be our servants." In verse 10 he said, "I *defy* the armies of Israel this day." In verse 11 — "When Saul and Israel heard those *words* of the Philistine, they were dismayed and greatly afraid." So this was the setting — the armies of God were paralyzed by the words of the giant.

God needed a man who was filled with His Word to go against Goliath, but there was none there, not even Saul, the King. So, back at the ranch, God moved upon Jesse to send his son, David, to check on his other sons who, at this time, were in Saul's army.

David left the sheep with a keeper. His mission was to bring some parched corn and homemade bread to his brothers (cookies from home) and to take some special cheese to the captain and also get news as to how his three brothers were doing. At this time the giant had been presenting himself for 40 days, every morning and every evening.

When David arrived on the scene, the giant came out again as David talked with his brothers. Verse 23 says that the giant spoke according to the same *words* and *DAVID HEARD THEM*. God's man was on the scene. Were not all the men present servants of God? What made the difference in David's life? The answer is this. David had filled his heart with the *WORD* of God. While he was keeping sheep, can you picture David with his harp, "speaking to yourselves in psalms and hymns and spiritual songs, singing and making melody in your hearts to the Lord" (Eph. 5:19)?

David had built himself up by singing words of the Holy Spirit to himself (FAITH COMES BY HEARING, Rom. 10:17).

When David then heard the words of Goliath he could not accept them. These words could not enter his heart because God's Word was in his heart. These words of unbelief just bounced off of David; he would not accept them or the fear that they generated. Remember that for 40 days, Saul and his whole army were terrified by Goliath. The Word of God in your heart is your protection against the giant attacks of Satan. You may rebuke Satan in the Name of Jesus, but unless you *KNOW*, unless you *KNOW* in your *HEART* that you *have authority* in the Name of Jesus, you will become fearful also. Thus, the end-time teaching ministry—to get God's word instead of your church's doctrine into your heart.

David could not help but ask, "Who is this?" The men told him of the situation and that King Saul had a reward offered to the man that would kill the giant. The reward was to marry the King's daughter and make his father's house free in Israel.

David wanted a double take and asked, "Would you repeat that, please?" For who is this uncircumcised Philistine, that he should defy the armies of the living God?

David's older brothers immediately became angry with him, and asked, ''With whom hast thou left the sheep, why did you come here? We know what you really wanted to do, just to see the battle.''

But David said, (verse 29), ''What have I done? Is there not a cause?'' David continued to pursue the matter. Verse 31, ''And when the *words* were heard that David spoke, they rehearsed them before King Saul, and he sent for him.'' David said, ''Let no man's heart fail because of him, I will go and fight this giant.'' But Saul warned David that he was not able because he was just a teenager and the giant was a trained man of war.

In the *natural,* this was true, but God's Word is *supernatural* and we have been called to a supernatural life, and overcoming life. Who is he that overcometh? He that believeth.

David had no doubt or fear that God would not back him up. He remembered the victories in his life and reported about the lion and bear that came to steal a lamb. Of the lion, David said, ''I went out after him and took the lamb out of his mouth; when the lion turned on me, I caught him by the beard and slew him. I slew also the bear and this uncircumcised Philistine shall be as one of them, seeing he has defied the armies of the Living God.''

DAVID SPOKE IT—HE SPOKE HIS VIC-
TORY RIGHT THERE. Mark 11:23 says if you
can *say* it you *will have* it.

The account goes on as Saul puts his own armor
suit on David (still thinking in the natural), but
David could not use it. He was not making prep-
aration for a battle, he was planning on a VIC-
TORY.

When the two met for the showdown, the giant
laughed at David and was insulted that they should
send a *BOY* with a stick to fight him.

Goliath made one good confession in verse 44
but that was the last one he made. On the other
hand, we see in verses 45-57 that David overcame
Goliath's confession and made statements of his
own.

I Samuel 17:45-47, "Then said David to the
Philistine, 'Thou comest to me with a sword, and
with a spear, and with a shield: but I come to thee in
the name of the Lord of hosts, the God of the
armies of Israel, whom thou hast defied. This day
will the Lord deliver thee into mine hand; and I will
smite thee, and take thine head from thee; and I will
give the carcases of the host of the Philistines this
day unto the fowls of the air, and to the wild beasts
of the earth; that all the earth may know that there is
a God in Israel. And all this assembly shall know
that the Lord saveth not with sword and spear: for
the battle is the Lord's and he will give you into our

hands.' ''

The rest is history. The point we are making is this: you may speak your future. David *said* it before he did anything about it.

David evidently knew Isaiah 54:17: ''No weapon that is formed against thee shall prosper, and every tongue that shall rise against thee in judgment thou shalt condemn. This is the heritage of the servants of the Lord, and their righteousness is of me, saith the Lord.''

If you *know* this, then you can *speak* it. Determine in your own heart to *confess* the *word* of God over any and every situation, regardless of what the situation looks like—*SPEAK IT*. But do not speak negative or against God's Word, because what you say is what you get.

Mark 11:23—''For verily I say unto you, That whosoever shall say unto this mountain, be thou removed, and be thou cast into the sea; and shall not doubt in his heart, but shall believe that those things which he *saith* shall come to pass; he shall *have* whatsoever he *saith*.''

YOU SHALL HAVE WHATSOEVER YOU SAY—DO NOT BE HUNG BY YOUR TONGUE!!!!

Chapter XIII

Christian Curses

Can a Christian curse? *DOES* a Christian curse? The answer is "yes" to both questions.

Jesus cursed (not cussed). Mark 11:14 states that Jesus spoke to the fig tree, "No man eat fruit of thee hereafter forever." He spoke a curse to the tree. And in the morning they passed the fig tree again and saw that it was dried up, Peter said in verse 21, "Look, the tree that you cursed is withered away." *To curse* means to call evil or injury upon, to damn, to afflict, to doom by speaking. It means to *"pray against."*

In English we have two other words that mean the same as to curse. *Imprecate* means a calling down of calamity on someone or something. *Anathematize* strictly refers to a formal utterance of condemnation by ecclesiastical authority.

Now the opposite of this is *"to bless."* The power of our words gives us the authority to *bless* or *curse.* Every time you speak you are building up or tearing down—blessing or cursing. You have what you say.

In James 3:8-11 we see this: "The tongue is an unruly evil full of deadly poison, therewith we *bless* God and *curse* men." These things "ought not so to be. Does a fountain put forth at the same place sweet and bitter?" James said that these things ought not to be, but they were.

WHO HAVE YOU BEEN CURSING? Examine yourself—who or what have you been cursing?

Have you ever told your children, "You are getting worse as the days go by?" That's a Christian curse.

Have you ever said of someone who is always behind schedule, "They will be late for their own funeral." With you putting a curse like that on them, they can never rise to do better.

Are there people in your fellowship that seem to be a little below in common sense and having a hard time to get moving in the right direction? What are you saying about them? "Seems like ole *so & so* will always be the same." "Looks like old Joe and Mary will never make it." "They will never do any better." Let's quit cursing our brethren and start blessing them so they can come up. They are trying but our curses have been holding them down.

Even the government is under the attack of the church, and God has already told us to pray for those in positions of leadership. Proverbs 11:11 says, "By the *BLESSING* of the upright the city is exalted but it is overthrown by the mouth of the wicked."

The last time I sent my tax money to the government, I wrote a note with it saying that I bless the government of the United States in the Name of Jesus.

We can bless and curse, and *we do*. Let's choose good.

An acquaintance of mine, a minister of the Gospel, told me of the following incident. A man of about 30 years of age came to him and told him of what was happening in his life. He saw a certain person and saw a *white ball* of some kind in a kind of vision type thing. That person soon died. He saw other people later that were associated with this white ball. They all died one by one. At the time he told this, he saw no more white balls and people, but he saw a white horizon and no one. But the thought that kept coming to him was that he personally could not cross this horizon. He received this as doom for his life. He was under a curse. *He died*. He had said, "I cannot get over this horizon." He was hung by his tongue.

Voodoo people as in south Louisiana and Haiti have used the curse. We Christians have learned that we can *bless* and *curse*. The opening of my mouth shall be right things—I'll bless people and only curse those things that will steal, kill, and destroy as in John 10:10.

One brother told me as we were preparing to

start a worship service, "The enemy is against us." That did not set right with me. I just suddenly spoke back, "I am against him also." I am against the devil and I'm for God; and that means more to me than knowing that he is against me. We have the power of life and death; the devil has only the power of death and Jesus overcame that.

Chapter XIV

Correct Tense

Romans 4:17 states that God calls those things that be not as though they *were*.

God speaks of the non-existent things as if they already existed. He spoke of Isaac being born to Abraham twenty-five years *before* it happened.

In Isaiah 9:6 the prophet spoke, "Unto us a child *is* born, unto us a son *is given*." This was spoken 700 years *before* it actually happened where they could see it with the *natural eye*.

FAITH calls it as done before it can be seen. FAITH is ACTING like God told you the truth.

You do not have to *see* it to know that you *possess* it. To receive the answer, accept it as already done; and do not let your confession put it in the future—put it in PAST TENSE. It has been done! Romans 8:37 says, *"Amid* all these things, we *are* more than conquerors." Is it when we are *out* of all these things? *No!!* "Nay, in all things we are more than conquerors through Him that loved us." I Peter 2:24 says, "By whose stripes you *WERE* healed." If I *WERE* then I *IS*.

Notice that in Philippians 4:19 Paul says, "My God *shall* supply all *your* need." But when he spoke of his *own self*, he always put the language in present tense—(verse 18) "I have all," "I am full"; (verse 13) "I can do all things"; (I Cor. 2:16) "We *have* the mind of Christ." He expects you to confess for yourself. Call those things that be not as though they were, *BEFORE* the natural eye can see them.

I AM JUSTIFIED BY THE WORDS OF MY MOUTH!! Many times a person will move the mountain according to Mark 11:23, but then move *other* mountains *into* their path by *other* negative speaking.

What is the use of clearing the path of garbage and then cluttering it again with *OTHER* garbage?

Please realize what God is saying to us about the *POWER* of our tongue—AMEN!!!

RESUME

REV. FRANCIS MARTIN is a deep South Louisiana "CAJUN", born the tenth child of French parents in the small town of Baldwin on Thanksgiving Day of 1938.

Baldwin is located on the Old Spanish Trail, a ridge of land about 6 miles wide bordering the Atchafalaya Cypress Swamp on the north, and the watery grass marsh on the south that flows into the Gulf of Mexico.

Having been raised in that land's strict Catholicism, Francis married a Baptist girl, Barbara Hanberry of Natchez, Mississippi. In 1956, she moved to Baldwin with her uncle and his family where he had assumed the pastorate of the newly organized Baptist mission.

In the spring of 1962, at the age of twenty-three, after five years of marriage, and the birth of three daughters, Francis was born again by the power of God's Word.

He experienced ten years of spiritual growth in the Baptist church. After the church became spirit filled with the evidence of speaking in tongues, the church was asked to remove the name "Baptist" from their sign.

In 1974, he moved fifty miles northwest to Lafayette and entered the Bible Teaching Ministry full time. His first assignments were in Branch, Louisiana and the Charismatic Teaching Center in Lafayette.

He authored four books while doing extensive traveling and teaching. On July 6, 1980, Francis started a local church, Family Life Christian Fellowship in Lafayette. In January 2002, he set in his protégé and under-study of fifteen years, Todd Menard as pastor. Francis assumed the position of overseer.

After being found in many extremes on his way here, Francis believes that he has reached a healthy place of balance to serve the body of Christ. Those extremes were devout Catholicism, Baptist Fundamentalism, Loose Chrismania, and Right-Wing Ultra Faithism. Family Life is non-denominational, fellowshipping with other churches as they allow.

Write or call for Other Offers

Cajun Praise: A worship CD in the traditional French music style of the local Cajuns - a very joyous album even if you do not speak Cajun.

A. **"The Couples Class"**– A nine CD series of comprehensive solutions to a variety of marriage situations, even yours.

B. The book, "The Kingdom's Economy" will be available about 1,1,11 by Tate Publishers of Tulsa OK. Call them or visit Amazon.com, your favorite book store, or the Author.

This message addresses Biblical giving for the Christian and financing of the Church without "Fund Raisers". A great gift for your Pastor.